Contents

G000149174

Foreword

Irish farmhouse cheeses with over fifty varieties made with the highest quality ingredients are used in these recipes. Each cheese is particular to its maker and reflects the unique environment in which it is produced.

The makers and their cheeses are diverse, offering a range of taste to suit every palate. Combining creativity and innovation, with respect for traditional craft and simplicity, Irish cheese makers are at the forefront of a new and exciting food culture.

Many of these recipes have been suggested by the cheese makers themselves. We hope that you will enjoy them with family and friends.

Michael Duffy, CEO
Bord Bia – Irish Food Board

Introduction

The revival of Irish farmhouse cheesemaking in the late 1970s has inspired a wide range of cheeses which have won considerable international acclaim. The role of Bord Bia in bringing these cheeses to all parts of the world has been crucial. It is particularly appropriate that their financial sponsorship should make possible the publication of the first book entirely devoted to recipes using Irish farmhouse cheese. The majority of the recipes have been handpicked from those provided by cheese makers, chefs and friends, and there are also several of my own favourites. I am deeply grateful for all the enthusiastic help and support I have been given.

The cheeses come from some of the most dramatic countryside in Ireland. As Giana Ferguson, who makes Gubbeen, has written, 'The key to great farm cheesemaking is for the cheese maker to use his or her talent to bring something of the flavour of the land, the *terroir*, to the cheese. As another fermentation process, cheesemaking is similar to winemaking – the herds are carefully chosen breeds of cows, goats or sheep, and they are the vines.' The cheeses are available in good cheesemongers, and, in particular, Sheridan's Cheesemongers in Dublin and Manning's Emporium in Ballylickey have provided me with cheese of particularly outstanding quality.

My love of good food developed while I grew up with my grandparents in a house in County Tipperary, where the food was always superb, and also during memorable travels with them to France and Italy at an early age, when I acquired a taste for good cheese. Living in West Cork, where the local convivium of the Slow Food Movement thrives and where many great Irish farmhouse cheeses are made, has been a great help in writing this book. I hope you enjoy the recipes, and are inspired to create some of your own using Irish farmhouse cheese.

Notes

BAKE BLIND To bake 'blind', line the bottom and sides of a quiche or tart case containing the uncooked pastry with baking paper and dried beans or rice. Bake at 180°C/350°F/Gas Mark 4 for 8–10 minutes, remove from the oven, discard the baking paper and beans or rice. When the pastry has cooled, it is ready for its filling.

CREAM There is only one middle-fat content cream available in Ireland. If using cream outside Ireland, use whipping cream or a half-and-half mix of single and double cream.

HERBS Use fresh herbs wherever possible, and if using dried herbs halve the quantity required for fresh herbs. If using fresh herbs, where dried herbs are specified, double the quantity.

SERVINGS The number of servings is stated in some recipes. In others, it is a question of personal judgement and appetite, deliberately left unspecified to preserve the original character of the recipe.

Tips for Cooking Cheese

1. Be careful not to add too much salt when cooking cheese, since most cheeses are perfectly salted.
2. Grate cheese just before you need it or it will lose its flavour. Cheese will grate more easily when cold. Grate hard cheese finely for adding to cooked dishes.
3. Do not apply heat to cheese for too long.

4. Only cook cheese in soup for long enough to melt the cheese.
5. It is best to remove cheese from the fridge an hour before cooking or serving in order to bring it to room temperature to bring out the flavour.

Tips for Storing Cheese

1. Always ask your cheese shop for advice on buying cheese and storing it.
2. If intending to eat your cheese on the day of purchase, do not refrigerate, but keep at room temperature.
3. It is very important to keep flies away from cheese.
4. Keep cheese wrapped in waxed paper. Blue cheeses can also be wrapped in foil. Hard cheese is best kept wrapped in a clean damp muslin cloth. It is important to wrap the exposed cut surfaces of hard cheeses. Waxed paper and clingfilm can also be used. If using clingfilm, be careful not to smother the rind of hard cheeses. Hard cheese can be kept wrapped in a damp cloth under a dampened earthenware flower pot.
5. The vegetable compartment of the fridge is the best place to keep your cheese, stored in a separate container from other foods, and with the lid unsealed.
6. If you have a large piece of cheese and you do not intend to eat it all, cut off a piece to eat, and keep the rest wrapped in the fridge.

Tapas

Giana Ferguson's Smoked Gubbeen Tapas

Serves 4

 4 slices of pumpernickel or German black bread (Available in
 most supermarkets. If bought from a baker, it must be thin
 and cut into neat rectangles.)
 60 ml/4 tbsp Smoked Gubbeen or other mild smoked cheese,
 grated
 1 tsp of butter
 pine nuts

Mix the butter with the grated cheese and spread quite gener-
ously to the centre of the pumpernickel bread. Top with a sprinkling of pine nuts and grill gently for 2 minutes until the nuts just
begin to brown and the cheese is melted. Eat immediately. This
works wonderfully as a lunch with a rocket salad and a glass
of beer.

Cratloe Hills Sheep's Cheese in Puff Pastry Wraps

Serves 8

 115 g/4 oz Cratloe Hills sheep's cheese
 350 g/12 oz frozen puff pastry

Defrost pastry. Cut cheese into 24 bite-size cubes. Roll out
pastry using a little flour. Use a pastry cutter to cut pastry
into squares. Wrap each cube of cheese in a pastry square,
then place on a floured baking tray. Brush with milk and bake
in an oven 200°C/400°F/gas mark 6 for about 18–20 minutes
until nicely browned.

 To serve as finger food, place a cocktail stick in each cube
before serving.

Grapes Stuffed with Boilie Cheese

Serves 6

    24 large dessert grapes
    6 balls of Boilie cows' or goats' cheese or 6 tbsp other soft
        goats' cheese

Remove pips from large dessert grapes. Stuff with Boilie cheese and reshape. Chill until about to serve.

Soft Goats' Cheese with Devil's Tongues

Serves 4

    4 red peppers
    225 g/8 oz Ardsallagh soft goats' cheese or other creamy soft
        goats' cheese
    olive oil
    salt and pepper

Cut peppers into quarters and remove core and seeds. Grill until the skin blackens. Place into a plastic bag until cool and the skins will then peel off easily. Cut the quarters in strips and place a small teaspoon of soft cheese at the end. Roll up the strips and arrange in a serving dish, end on, like little roses. Drizzle a little olive oil over the dish and season with salt. Serve as a starter with a little green salad or as a side dish with cold meats.

Blue Cheese Stuffed with Dates and Prunes

Serves 6

    55 g/2 oz Cashel Blue, Crozier Blue or other blue cheese
    25 g/1 oz soft butter
    10 ml/2 tsp Irish whiskey
    24 dates or prunes that do not need soaking

Mash the cheese and batter together and then incorporate the whiskey. Chill the mixture for 40 minutes. Remove the stones from the dates or prunes. With a teaspoon, stuff the dates or prunes with some of the cheese mixture. Chill in the fridge for an hour before serving.

Cheese Straws

Makes 40

115 g/4 oz plain flour, sifted
70 g/2½ oz butter
small pinch of salt
pinch of cayenne pepper
55 g/2 oz Knockanore, Baylough, Mount Callan, Hegarty
*   Farmhouse Cheddar or other semi-hard cheese*
30 ml/2 tbsp whisked egg

Add the salt and cayenne pepper to the flour in a bowl. Add the butter gradually to the flour mixture and rub into the flour until the mixture looks like breadcrumbs. Then, mix in the cheese. Pour in the whisked egg, and cut it through the mixture with a knife. Knead and form into a ball, and roll out on a floured board to a thickness of 6 mm/¼ in. Cut into 40 even-sized strips and place apart from each other on a greased and lightly floured baking tray and cook in a preheated oven at 190°C/375°F/gas mark 5 for 15–18 minutes until golden brown. Serve warm.

Soups

Leek, Bacon, Cheese and Potato Soup

Serves 4

30 ml/2 tbsp olive oil
150 g/5½ oz leeks, thinly sliced
4 rashers smoked back bacon, rind removed and chopped
300 g/10½ oz peeled potatoes, cut into small cubes
850 ml/1½ pt chicken stock
55 g/2 oz Hegarty Farmhouse Cheddar or other semi-hard
*   cheese*
freshly ground black pepper

Warm some olive oil in a saucepan and add the bacon and leeks. Fry gently until cooked, but not browned. Add the stock and potatoes, bring to the boil and simmer for 35 minutes. Add cheese and cook, stirring well for one minute until just melted. Remove from heat. Season with black pepper and serve immediately.

Cashel Blue and Celery Soup

Serves 4

    350 g/12 oz celery, washed, trimmed and chopped
    1.2 l/2 pt chicken or vegetable stock
    55 g/2 oz Cashel Blue or other blue cheese
    60 ml/4 tbsp cream
    freshly ground black pepper

Place the celery and stock in a saucepan, cover, bring to the boil and simmer for 45 minutes. Strain off the liquid and reserve. Put the celery through a food processor, then return to the pan with the reserved liquid. Warm, then add the cheese through a sieve and the cream. Remove from heat, season with black pepper and serve.

Blue Cheese, Bacon and Courgette Soup

Serves 4–6

    a little olive oil
    6 streaky rashers, chopped
    1 onion, chopped
    2 large courgettes, sliced
    6 medium potatoes, peeled and cubed
    1.1 l/2 pt chicken or vegetable stock
    85 g/3 oz Crozier Blue or other blue cheese
    125 ml/4 fl oz cream
    black pepper
    2 tbsp parsley, finely chopped

Sauté bacon for a few minutes in a little oil. Remove a few pieces of bacon for final garnish. Add the onion, courgette and potatoes. Cover the pan and cook gently for about 10 minutes. Stir in the stock and simmer for another 15 minutes or until the potatoes are soft. Remove from the heat and put the soup through a blender or food processor. Return to the saucepan. Stir in the cheese and cream and heat gently. Add the reserved bacon, black pepper and parsley and serve.

Cheese and Spring Onion Soup

Serves 4

>   25 g/1 oz butter
>   4 spring onions, trimmed and finely sliced
>   25 g/1 oz flour
>   600 ml/1 pint milk
>   300 ml/½ pint chicken stock
>   salt and freshly ground black pepper
>   115 g/4 oz Baylough farmhouse cheese or other semi-hard
>   cheese, grated
>   2 tbsp chopped fresh parsley
>   freshly ground black pepper

Melt the butter in a large saucepan and lightly fry the spring onions, without browning. Add flour and cook for 2 minutes. Gradually beat in the milk, stock and seasonings. Heat, whisking continuously, until soup comes to the boil and thickens. Simmer for 5 minutes. Remove soup from heat and stir in the cheese. Pour into warmed soup bowls and garnish with parsley and pepper.

Starters

Coolea and Leek Fritters

Serves 8

> 400 g/14 oz leek, very thinly sliced
> 25 g/1 oz butter
> 200 g/7 oz flour
> 2 free range eggs
> 250 ml/9 fl oz milk
> 200 g/7 oz mature Coolea farmhouse cheese, freshly grated
>   or other semi-hard cheese
> salt and freshly ground pepper
> 1 fresh red chilli pepper, deseeded and finely chopped
> freshly grated nutmeg
>
> tomato dip:
> 8 tomatoes, peeled, deseeded and finely chopped
> 4 tbsp fresh basil leaves, chopped or 30 ml/2 tbsp pesto
>   sauce
> 150 ml/¼ pt extra virgin olive oil
> salt and freshly ground black pepper

Melt the butter, add the thinly sliced leeks, cover and sweat on a gentle heat until soft, but not coloured (approximately 5 minutes). Cool for 40 minutes. Meanwhile make the tomato dip by putting the tomatoes, basil or pesto and oil in a bowl and mixing thoroughly. Season with salt and freshly ground black pepper. Then sieve the flour into a bowl, make a well in the centre, add in the eggs and break up with a whisk. Add the milk gradually, whisking all the time in a circular movement from the centre to the outside of the bowl. Add the leeks, when cool, and the grated cheese and red chilli pepper. Season with salt, freshly ground pepper and nutmeg to taste. Heat a frying pan, preferably non-stick, on a medium heat. Drop a tablespoon of the batter onto the pan, allow to cook until golden on one side, flip over onto the other and cook for a moment or two more. Taste and correct the seasoning if necessary. Serve hot with the tomato dip.

Smoked Salmon and Soft Goats' Cheese

Serves 3–4

> *12 slices of smoked salmon*
> *225 g/8 oz Ardsallagh soft goats' cheese or other creamy soft*
> *   goats' cheese*
> *1 shredded lettuce*
> *1 lemon*
> *capers*
> *brown soda bread*

Take thinly sliced portions of salmon and place a wedge of cheese at one side. Roll the smoked salmon into a cone so that the cheese is peeping out. Dress the plates sparsely with lettuce and arrange 3 or 4 cones per person. Garnish with lemon quarters and sprinkle with capers. Serve with fingers of brown soda bread. This is ideal as a Christmas Day starter.

Deep-fried St Killian

Serves 3

> *1 St Killian or other Camembert-type cheese*
> *1 egg, beaten*
> *breadcrumbs*
> *redcurrant jelly or cranberry sauce*

Cut the St Killian into wedges (2.5 cm–4 cm/1–1½ in. thick). Do not remove white crust. Dip wedges into the beaten egg and then into the breadcrumbs. Repeat the process. Place in the refrigerator for about half an hour. Deep-fry wedges in hot oil for about one minute. Drain well. Serve immediately with hot toast (crusts removed) and redcurrant jelly or cranberry sauce.

Clonakilty Blackpudding Stuffed with Smoked Gubbeen

Serves 2

225 g/8 oz Clonakilty Blackpudding
70 g/2½ oz Smoked Gubbeen cheese
1 egg
plain flour to coat
breadcrumbs to coat
sunflower oil for frying

Peel both the black pudding and the cheese. Break up each of them and keep separate. Place half the black pudding between two sheets of clingwrap and flatten out into a sheet. Do the same with separate clingwrap to the remaining black pudding. Make a tight ball with half the cheese. Remove the clingwrap from the top of one sheet of the black pudding. Place the cheese in the centre and pull the pudding into a ball around the cheese manipulating it with your hands to seal it firmly all the way round. Follow the same process with the remaining cheese and sheet of black pudding. Beat the egg. Coat the balls of black pudding and cheese with flour, then with beaten egg and breadcrumbs. Heat a layer of sunflower oil about 2.5 cm/1 in. deep in a frying pan. Fry the breadcrumbed balls until they are golden brown and cooked through. Serve with a little side salad and West Cork Herb Farm Red Pepper Relish or a tablespoon of apple sauce.

Bantry Bay Scallops

Serves 4

    8 large scallops
    8 slices streaky bacon, rind removed
    55 g/2 oz Durrus or Gubbeen, grated
    1 clove of garlic, chopped
    oil and butter for frying
    4 handfuls of dressed lettuce leaves

Wrap scallops in streaky bacon. Sauté in oil and butter with the garlic for 2 minutes on each side or until cooked. Remove from pan, sprinkle with the grated cheese and place under a hot grill until the cheese is melting and beginning to brown. Serve immediately on the dressed lettuce leaves.

(courtesy of James Hegarty of Bantry, Co. Cork)

Gortnamona Goats' Cheese Baskets

Serves 4

    190 g/6½ oz Gortnamona cheese or other soft goats' cheese
    8 tomatoes
    85 g/3 oz crème fraîche
    2 tbsp chopped chives
    1 tsp chopped basil

Wash and dry tomatoes. Slice off the top of each tomato and scoop out pulp. Lightly salt the inside of each tomato and turn over to drain. Mix cheese, crème fraîche, chives and basil in a bowl and fill the tomatoes with the mixture. Sprinkle with chopped chives and replace the caps over the cheese. Serve immediately on a bed of tossed leaves.

Crozier Blue Cheese Mousse

Serves 4

    1 tsp powdered gelatine
    15 ml/1 tbsp water

175 g/6 oz Crozier Blue or other blue cheese
2 eggs
cayenne pepper
15 ml/1 tbsp fresh lemon juice
150 ml/¼ pt fresh cream

Put the tablespoon of water in a mug or cup, sprinkle the powdered gelatine over it and leave to swell. Separate the eggs. Place the egg yolks, cheese, lemon juice and a pinch of cayenne pepper in a bowl and beat together thoroughly with a hand whisk. Add the cream and go on beating until the mixture is thick. Dissolve the gelatine, stirring over a pan of hot water, then stir it into the cheese mixture. Whisk the egg whites until they are stiff and fold into the cheese mixture with a metal spoon. Fill four ramekin dishes with the mixture and allow to chill until set in the fridge. To serve, decorate with a sprig of watercress and a slice of lemon, and accompany with toast and butter.

Ardrahan Filo Baskets in Blackcurrant Sauce

Serves 4

225 g/8 oz Ardrahan cheese or other washed-rind cheese
4 sheets filo pastry
1 egg, beaten

for the sauce:
350 g/12 oz blackcurrants
115 g/4 oz granulated sugar

(If blackcurrants are unavailable, make a sauce with blackcurrant jam by gently heating and adding a little water. Omit the sugar.)

Roll out the 4 sheets of pastry. Cut the cheese into 4 pieces and place in the centre of each pastry sheet. Gather the 4 corners of each of the pastries together to make a basket shape. Brush with beaten egg, then bake in the oven for 20 minutes at 180°C/350°F/gas mark 4. Meanwhile, prepare the blackcurrant sauce. Cook the blackcurrants with the granulated sugar and put through a blender or food processor. Rub the mixture through a sieve to remove the seeds. Serve the filo baskets with the warm blackcurrant sauce.

Snacks

Cheese, Tomato and Onion Savoury

Serves 2

> 15 ml/1 tbsp olive oil or 15 g/½ oz butter
> 55 g/2 oz onion, finely sliced
> 150 g/5½ oz tomatoes, sliced
> 55 g/2 oz Hegarty Farmhouse Cheddar or other semi-hard
>   cheese, grated
> pinch of sugar
> salt and freshly ground black pepper
> 2 slices of hot buttered toast

Heat the oil or butter in a pan and gently fry the chopped onion until tender. Add the tomato slices, sugar and seasoning according to taste. When the tomatoes are soft, stir in the cheese, and continue to stir until it melts. Serve immediately on top of the hot buttered toast.

(courtesy of Myrtle Allen of Ballymaloe House)

Grilled Ciabatta with Olive and Goats' Cheese

Serves 4–6

> Black olive tapenade:
> 3 cloves garlic
> 250 g/9 oz good quality stoned black olives

2 tsp capers
25 g/1 oz sundried tomatoes, chopped
pinch of cayenne pepper
150 ml/¼ pt olive oil

1 large ciabatta loaf
60 ml/4 tbsp olive tapenade
150 g/5½ oz fresh young Oisin goats' cheese or other soft
*   goats' cheese*

To make the tapenade, put everything except the oil in a food
processor and blend to a coarse purée, then add the oil and
blend again briefly. Store the tapenade in an airtight container with a thin layer of olive oil above the purée, preferably in
the fridge, and it will keep for weeks. Cut the ciabatta in half
lengthways, spread a thin layer of tapenade on both halves,
drizzle some olive oil over that and lay some thin slices of
goats' cheese on top. Place under a hot grill until the cheese
starts to brown. Cut into chunks and share it out.

*From The Café Paradiso Cookbook by Denis Cotter published by
Atrium in 1999. Denis Cotter is chef/proprietor of the Café Paradiso
in Cork.*

Irish Rarebit

Serves 2

15 g/½ oz butter
85 g/3 oz smoked Knockanore cheese or other lightly
*   smoked cheese*
2.5 ml/½ tsp Lakeshore Strong Irish Mustard
10 ml/2 tsp Irish whiskey or 15 ml/1 tbsp Guinness
salt
pepper
1 egg yolk
2 slices of bread

Melt the butter in a small saucepan. Add the cheese,
whiskey, mustard, salt and pepper, and stir over a low heat,
until the cheese has melted. Draw off the heat, and beat in

the egg yolk. Toast the bread on one side under a hot grill. Remove from heat and spoon the mixture onto the untoasted side of the bread. Place under a high heat to brown quickly and serve at once.

Baked Gubbeen with Thyme and Rosemary

Serves 4

  450 g/1 lb wheel of Gubbeen
  1 tbsp chopped mixed thyme and rosemary or other herbs
  2 cloves of garlic, chopped
  black pepper
  crusty loaf of bread

Preheat the oven to 180°C/350°F/gas mark 4, cut the cheese in half horizontally to make 2 rounds. Sprinkle the black pepper, herbs and chopped garlic on the bottom half of the cheese. Replace the top disc of cheese and place the wheel onto aluminium foil. Wrap the foil around the cheese, forming a chimney hole on top with the excess foil. The chimney lets out the moisture while the cheese bakes. Lay the cheese on a baking sheet and bake for 20 minutes or until soft and runny. Spread on slices of chunky bread while the cheese is still warm.

Barbecued Corleggy

Serves 4

  350 g/12 oz Corleggy, Drumlin or other hard cheese
  rosemary, thyme
  fresh pink peppercorns
  a little extra virgin olive oil

Cut the cheese across the middle like a bread roll. Put the rosemary, thyme, fresh pink peppercorns according to taste and a little olive oil between the two halves of the cheese. Wrap in aluminium foil and cook for 7–10 minutes on a good barbecue or in an oven 200°C/400°F/gas mark 6. To serve, unwrap foil, open and spoon out to eat with crusty bread.

Blue Cheese and Walnut Pittas

Makes 8

> 125 g/4½ oz celery, thinly sliced
> 55 g/2 oz walnuts, chopped
> 85 g/3 oz sultanas
> pinch of grated nutmeg
> 30 ml/2 tbsp mayonnaise
> 15 ml/1 tbsp natural yoghurt
> 45 ml/3 tbsp tahini (sesame paste)
> 1.25 ml/¼ tsp runny honey
> 1 large ripe pear, sliced
> 8 small pitta breads
> shredded iceberg lettuce
> 90 g/3¼ oz Cashel Blue or other blue cheese, rind removed
>   and crumbled

Mix together celery, walnuts, sultanas, pears and nutmeg. Combine mayonnaise, tahini, honey and half the cheese to make a smooth consistency. Mix in with fruit and nut mixture and lightly season. Lightly toast pittas. Split along one side, place a little lettuce in the pocket and top with the cheese, nut and fruit cream. Cover with the remaining cheese. Serve immediately.

Gortnamona and Strawberry Croissants

> 4 warm croissants or bagels
> Gortnamona goats' cheese or other soft goats' cheese
> soft butter
> 225 g/8 oz strawberries

Halve the croissants and spread them with butter. Slice the Gortnamona and place in croissant. Layer the strawberries on the cheese, close croissant and serve.

County Cork Salami Snack

Irish soda bread
soft butter
slices of Krawczyk's West Cork salami
slices of Natural Carrigaline, Gubbeen, Ardrahan, Durrus or
Milleens

Lay slices of salami on buttered bread and top with slices of
cheese with rind removed.

Tomato, Aubergine, Cheese and Ham Crostini

4 slices of ciabatta bread or French bread
virgin olive oil for drizzling
2 ripe vine tomatoes, cut into fine dice
55 g/2 oz sliced ham
4 slices of aubergine, fried and kept warm
55 g/2 oz slices of Durrus, Gubbeen, Ardrahan or Smoked
Knockanore cheese, rind removed

Toast ciabatta bread or French bread. Drizzle with olive oil,
cover with diced tomato, then slices of ham and then fried
aubergine, top with slices of cheese and place under hot
grill until cheese is melting and beginning to brown. Serve
immediately.

Cheese and Onion Crostini

Serves 2

1 small French bread stick
olive oil
55 g/2 oz Dunbarra plain or Natural Carrigaline, crumbed
1 small red onion, sliced into half rings
25 g/1 oz light brown sugar
knob of butter
seasoning

Cut French stick into slices about 12.5 mm/½ in. thick. Lay on baking tray, drizzle with olive oil. Bake in oven set at 190°C/375°F/gas mark 5 until golden brown. Allow to cool completely. Melt butter and cook onion for 2 minutes. Sprinkle the sugar and season. Continue to cook on medium heat until sugar is caramelized. Spoon the mixture onto bread and sprinkle over the cheese. Grill until cheese is golden brown and bubbling.

Clonmore Gouda Goats' Cheese Snack

Serves 1

> 1 large breakfast mushroom
> 25 g/1 oz Clonmore Gouda goats' cheese or Oisin Gouda goats' cheese
> salt and black pepper
> 5 ml/1 tsp soya sauce (optional)
> 1 slice of toast

Peel mushroom and sprinkle with soya sauce. Season with salt and black pepper. Cook under medium grill until soft. Place mushroom on the toast and scatter with cheese. Grill until lightly browned. Serve immediately.

Wicklow Blue, Bacon, Mayonnaise and Watercress Baguette

Serves 2

> 1 thin French bread stick
> 30 ml/2 tbsp mayonnaise
> 2 handfuls of watercress
> 175 g/6 oz Wicklow Blue or Abbey Blue Brie, cut in slices
> 6 warm grilled slices of streaky bacon, rind removed and cut up

Cut the French stick in half lengthways. Spread the mayonnaise on the bottom half, and arrange the watercress on top. Cover with the slices of cheese, then the cut-up bacon. Replace the top half of the French stick, and cut into two. Serve immediately.

Salmon and Dilliskus Cheese Baguette

Serves 2

> *2 small French bread sticks*
> *225 g/8 oz cooked fresh salmon, skin and bone removed or 4
>   slices Irish smoked salmon*
> *30 ml/2 tbsp mayonnaise*
> *juice of a quarter of a lemon*
> *salt and freshly ground pepper*
> *freshly chopped dill*
> *115 g/4 oz Dilliskus cheese, sliced*

Mix the lemon juice with the mayonnaise. Add the lemon mayonnaise to the salmon and mix lightly in a bowl, season with salt and pepper and add a little dill. Cut the baguette in half and spread the salmon mixture on the lower half. Top with slices of Dilliskus cheese and then replace the upper half of the baguette.

Salads

Blue Cheese Dressing

> *55 g/2 oz blue cheese, either Cashel Blue, Bellingham Blue
>   or Crozier Blue work well*
> *75 ml/5 tbsp olive oil*
> *15 ml/1 tbsp balsamic vinegar*
> *5 ml/1 tsp Lakeshore Strong Irish Mustard*
> *salt and freshly ground pepper*

Crumble the blue cheese and keep separate. Whisk the oil, vinegar and mustard together, add the blue cheese and season with salt and pepper.

O'Connell's Warm Salad of Gubbeen Cheese and Fingal Ferguson's Gubbeen Bacon

Serves 6

15 ml/1 tbsp olive oil
350 g/12 oz streaky Gubbeen bacon or other streaky bacon
6 handfuls of mixed green leaves
55 g/2 oz Gubbeen cheese or similar cheese, diced

dressing:
45 ml/3 tbsp sunflower oil
45 ml/3 tbsp olive oil
5 ml/1 tsp of Lakeshore Whole Grain Mustard or other whole
    grain mustard
30 ml/2 tbsp Fruit of the Vine Cider Vinegar or other cider
    vinegar
salt, pepper and sugar

Heat a frying pan and add a little olive oil. When it is smoking, add the lardons of bacon and fry until crisp. While the bacon is cooking, put all the ingredients for the dressing in a bowl and whisk with a fork. Toss the leaves in the dressing and divide between six hot plates. The leaves should be just glistening with the dressing. Sprinkle the cubes of cheese around the leaves and finally the bacon straight from the pan. Serve immediately.

(courtesy of Rory O'Connell at Ballymaloe House)

Beetroot, Goats' Cheese and Walnut Salad

Serves 4

a selection of salad leaves
115 g/4 oz St Tola or Ardsallagh or other soft goats' cheese
3 beetroots, cooked
10–15 walnuts, coarsely chopped

dressing:
15 ml/1 tbsp balsamic vinegar
45 ml/3 tbsp extra virgin olive oil
2.5 ml/½ tsp Dijon mustard

Wash and dry the salad leaves. Put a small handful of leaves onto each plate. Slice the goats' cheese and beetroot into wedges and place 2–3 of each onto each plate. Sprinkle the walnuts over the salads. Put all the ingredients for the dressing into a small bowl and mix with a spoon. Pour the dressing over the salads just before serving.

(courtesy of Clodagh McKenna)

Sweet Rocket Goats' Cheese Salad

Serves 4

> *225 g/8 oz Ardsallagh soft goats' cheese or other creamy soft goats' cheese*
> *4 handfuls of rocket leaves*
> *2 sprigs of fresh mint*
> *honey*

Wash rocket leaves and arrange on individual plates. Wash mint and tear into small pieces. Sprinkle a little on each plate. Slice well-chilled goats' cheese into thick slices and arrange over salad. Drizzle the honey over the whole dish. Serve as a starter or lunchtime snack.

Cabbage Salad with Blue Cheese

Serves 6–8

> *½ hard white or red cabbage*
> *4 parsley sprigs*
> *225 g/8 oz crisp apples*
> *100 g/3½ oz small carrots*
> *½ tsp of fresh thyme*
> *salt and black pepper to taste*
> *pinch of curry powder*
> *225 g/8 oz Cashel Blue or other blue cheese, rind removed*
> *65 ml/4¹/₃ tbsp yoghurt*
> *65 ml/4¹/₃ tbsp mayonnaise*

Shred the cabbage very finely. Soak it in cold water for 2 hours or longer, changing the water 2 or 3 times. Drain, and dry it well. Finely chop the parsley leaves. Peel and core the apples, and top and tail the carrots. Grate, not too finely, the apples and carrots. Combine the parsley, apples and carrots with the cabbage. Add the thyme leaves, seasoning and curry powder. Mix well. Cut the cheese into small cubes and fold them into the salad. Combine the yoghurt and mayonnaise and pour it over. Toss salad shortly before serving.

Boilie and Avocado Salad

Serves 4

4 small handfuls of lettuce leaves
1 ripe avocado, stone removed, peeled and cut into cubes
4 smoked bacon rashers, trimmed, cooked and chopped
12 balls of Boilie goats' cheese (1 × 200 g jar) or 115 g/4 oz
    Abbey St Canice or Waterford feta

dressing:
45 ml/3 tbsp lemon juice
45 ml/3 tbsp Boilie oil or other oil
5 ml/1 tsp caster sugar
salt and freshly ground white pepper
1 tbsp freshly chopped parsley

Arrange lettuce leaves on 4 serving plates. Place rashers and cheese on top. Sprinkle avocado cubes with a little lemon juice and place on plate. Place remaining lemon juice, oil, sugar, salt and a generous amount of freshly ground white pepper together in a bowl, beat well, and stir in parsley. Just before serving, sprinkle salad with the dressing. Serve with garlic bread.

Smoked Chicken, Ham and Cheese Salad

Serves 4

1 large iceberg lettuce
225 g/8 oz Ummera smoked chicken or other smoked chicken, cut in strips
225 g/8 oz cooked ham, cut in strips
225 g/8 oz Durrus or other washed-rind cheese, cut in strips or cubed
2 hard-boiled eggs, quartered
2 firm ripe tomatoes, quartered

dressing:
90 ml/6 tbsp cream
20 ml/4 tsp white wine vinegar
pinch of salt
45 ml/3 tbsp light olive oil
2 tbsp chopped chives
freshly ground black pepper

garlic croutons:
4 large slices of white bread, crusts removed, and cut into small squares
60 ml/4 tbsp oil
2 cloves of garlic, peeled and finely chopped

Wash and dry the lettuce. Break it into bite-sized pieces and line a large salad bowl to form a thick base for the other ingredients. Arrange the smoked chicken, ham and cheese pinwheel fashion around the centre, and the egg and tomato around the outside. Chill for at least 45 minutes before serving. Meanwhile, make the dressing and croutons. To make the dressing, put the cream, chopped chives, vinegar, salt and pepper in a small bowl or jug, and whisk for a minute until frothy. Still whisking, gradually add the oil, check the seasoning and chill until ready to serve. To make the croutons, heat the oil over a gentle heat. When hot, but not smoking, add the bread squares, and fry, turning them occasionally, until golden brown. About 2 minutes before the end of the cooking, add the garlic. Cook for a further 2 minutes. Remove the croutons, and drain on kitchen towel. To serve, remove the salad and dressing from the fridge, pour the dressing over the salad and sprinkle with the garlic croutons.

Ardrahan, Smoked Salmon, Quails' Eggs and Asparagus Salad

Serves 4

115 g/4 oz Ardrahan cheese, rind removed
225 g/8 oz Ummera smoked salmon or other Irish smoked salmon
12 quails' eggs
24 asparagus tips

dressing:
1 clove of garlic
15 ml/1 tbsp white wine vinegar
15 ml/1 tbsp lemon juice
5 ml/1 tsp Dijon mustard
90–120 ml/6–8 tbsp virgin olive oil
salt and freshly ground pepper
1 tbsp parsley

Boil the quails' eggs for 4 minutes. Cool, remove shells and cut in half. Cook the asparagus in boiling salted water for 12–15 minutes or until tender, drain in a colander, and run under cold water for 1 minute. Pat dry with a clean tea towel. Cut the cheese into 1.25 cm/½ in. cubes. Divide the smoked salmon and lay the slices on 4 small plates. Arrange 6 asparagus tips over the smoked salmon, then scatter with the cheese cubes and halved quails' eggs. Serve with the dressing. To make the dressing, peel the garlic, and crush with a pinch of salt. Place in a small bowl or jug and stir in the white wine vinegar, lemon juice and mustard until well blended. Gradually add in the olive oil with a small whisk or fork. Season with salt and freshly ground black pepper and parsley.

Egg Dishes

Individual Baked Eggs with Cheese

Serves 2 as a starter or 1 as a main course

2 eggs
butter for greasing
salt and freshly ground pepper
75 ml/5 tbsp cream
25 g/1 oz hard or semi-hard cheese, grated
freshly chopped parsley or chives

Preheat the oven to 180°C/350°F/gas mark 4. Grease two individual ramekin dishes, and warm them in the oven. Break one egg into each dish and season with salt and pepper. Place the dishes in a roasting tin and surround with boiling water to a level of halfway up the sides of the ramekins. Bake in the oven for about 6–8 minutes until the whites are set, but the yolks are still soft. Pour half the cream over each ramekin and top each one with half the cheese. Sprinkle with a little chopped parsley or chives. Cook for a further 3–4 minutes. To add interest to this dish, a little chopped fried streaky bacon, cooked spinach or chopped cooked mushrooms can be placed in each ramekin before adding the egg. When cooked, serve immediately.

Little St Gall Soufflés

Serves 4 as a starter

2 large eggs
75 ml/5 tbsp cream
115 g/4 oz St Gall, Mount Callan or Hegarty Farmhouse
    Cheddar, grated
a small pinch of cayenne pepper
salt and freshly ground pepper
15 g/½ oz breadcrumbs

Preheat the oven to 200°C/400°F/gas mark 6. Grease 4 ramekins with butter. Whisk the eggs well, and then mix in the cream. Reserve 15 g/½ oz of the cheese and put aside. Then add the rest to the eggs and cream. Add the cayenne, salt and pepper. Divide the mixture between the buttered dishes. Mix the reserved cheese and breadcrumbs and spoon over the soufflé mixture. Cook in the oven for 15–20 minutes until golden and risen. Serve immediately with teaspoons.

Blue Cheese and Mushroom Soufflé

Serves 4–6

    butter for greasing
    55 g/2 oz butter for soufflé
    70 g/2½ oz plain flour
    425 ml/¾ pt milk
    salt and freshly ground black pepper
    115 g/4 oz Cashel Blue with rind removed, crumbled or
        mashed
    4 egg yolks
    5 egg whites
    85 g/3 oz button mushrooms

Set the oven to 190°C/375°F/gas mark 5. Brush a little butter over the inside of a 1 litre (1¾ pt) soufflé dish. Melt the 55 g/2 oz butter in a medium-sized pan. Add the flour and stir over low heat for 2 minutes. Still stirring constantly, add the milk gradually and cook for another 3 minutes. The sauce will be very thick and should leave the sides of the pan cleanly. Turn sauce into a bowl. Beat in a little seasoning and the cheese, making sure that any lumps of cheese are beaten out, then beat in the egg yolks, one at a time, until fully blended. In a separate bowl, whisk the egg whites until firm. Stir one spoonful into the soufflé base mixture, then fold in the rest. Pour half the mixture gently into the prepared dish. Sprinkle with the mushrooms, then cover gently with the remaining soufflé mixture. Bake the soufflé for 35–40 minutes until it is well risen and browned. Serve immediately with a tossed green salad.

Tarts & Pizzas

Spinach and Durrus Cheese Pizza

Makes 4 pizzas

12 thin slices of Durrus cheese, rind removed
4 large handfuls of roughly chopped spinach
salt, pepper, freshly grated nutmeg
olive oil for drizzling

pizza dough:
500 g/1 lb 2 oz strong unbleached flour
7 g sachet of quick yeast
10 g/¼ oz sea salt
350 ml/12 fl oz approx. water

Heat oven to 220°C/425°F/gas mark 7 and put the baking tray in the oven to warm – this is essential for a crispy base. Mix the pizza dough ingredients together by hand in a bowl, or in a mixer. Knead for 4–5 minutes until a ball can be formed. Add a little flour, if necessary. Leave to rise for about 1½ hours in a warm place until doubled in size. Knock back, then divide into 4 pieces. To make each pizza, roll out a piece of pizza dough very thinly on a flour-dusted work top. Place on a baking tray. Top with the roughly chopped spinach. Season with salt, pepper and grated nutmeg. Arrange the slices of cheese on top. Drizzle with olive oil. Bake for 8–10 minutes until pastry is golden and crispy, and the cheese has melted.

(courtesy of the Good Things Cafe, Durrus, Co. Cork)

Clonakilty Blackpudding, Bacon and Goats' Cheese Pizza

Serves 1

  1 pizza base
  15 ml/1 tbsp tomato puree or 2–3 sliced tomatoes
  6 slices of Clonakilty Blackpudding, cooked and crumbled
  3 slices of bacon, diced and cooked
  55 g/2 oz of goats' cheese (sliced or grated)
  a few sprigs of thyme

Set the oven to 220°C/425°F/gas mark 7. Spread the tomato mixture over the pizza base. Sprinkle on the bacon, and lay on the Clonakilty black pudding, then the cheese and thyme. Bake for 10–15 minutes until crisp and the cheese has melted. Serve immediately.

Abbey Feta Cheese Quiche with Tomato, Basil and Aubergine

Serves 4

  300 g/10½ oz puff pastry
  400 g/14 oz beef tomatoes
  15 g/½ oz fresh basil
  325 g/11½ oz aubergines
  125 g/4½ oz Abbey St Canice feta cheese or Waterford feta
  250 ml/9 fl oz cream
  4 eggs
  pinch of salt and pepper

Roll out the pastry and line a 23 cm/9 in. circular quiche tin. Place some of the sliced tomato in a layer in the base of the tin. Season and sprinkle with basil. Cover with a layer of aubergine. Arrange the remaining beef tomato and feta cheese slices alternately in a circle around the edge of the tin. Place the remaining slices of aubergine in the centre overlapping in a circle. Whisk the cream and eggs together and pour into the quiche tin. Place in a preheat-ed oven and cook at 200°C/400°F/gas mark 6 for 45 min-utes. Serve warm or cold with relish or chutney.

(courtesy of Sarah Webb at the Gallic Kitchen)

Farmhouse Traditional Blue Cheese and Onion Tartlets

Serves 4

4 individual flan cases

pastry:
400 g/14 oz plain flour
200 g/7 oz butter
25 g/1 oz poppy seeds
cold water
pinch of salt

filling:
25 g/1 oz butter
300 g/10 oz onions, sliced
250 g/9 oz leeks, cut into thin rounds
250 g/9 oz Bellingham Blue cheese or other blue cheese
3 cloves of garlic
3 eggs
200 ml/7 fl oz cream
15 g/½ oz pine nuts
salt and freshly ground pepper

Make the pastry, adding the poppy seeds when the butter is rubbed in and bake blind. Cook the onion, garlic and leeks in a little butter until tender but not soft. Add the cheese to this mixture along with the salt and pepper. Whisk the eggs and cream together and add most of this to the mixture. Place the mixture in the pre-baked pastry cases and pour the remaining whisked egg and cream on top. Scatter with pine nuts and bake in an oven preheated to 190°C/375°F/gas mark 5 for approximately 30 minutes or until just set and browned on top.

Smoked Salmon and Goats' Cheese Tart

Serves 4

175 g/6 oz shortcrust pastry
175 g/6 oz Woodcock smoked salmon or any other good quality smoked salmon
2 tbsp fresh dill and basil
175 g/6 oz Blue bell goats' cheese or any other soft goats' cheese with the rind cut off
3 eggs
150 ml/¼ pt milk
salt and pepper

Roll out the shortcrust pastry to line a 20 mm/8 in. quiche dish. Bake blind for 12 minutes at 180°C/350°F/gas mark 4. Chop smoked salmon and arrange it around the pastry case. Scatter 2 tbsp of chopped fresh dill and basil over the smoked salmon. Mix the eggs and milk together with some freshly ground black pepper and a pinch of salt. Add the goats' cheese and mix with a fork. It will be lumpy, but do not worry. Pour into the pastry base over the smoked salmon and herbs. Cook at 170°C/325°F/gas mark 3 for 25–30 minutes until set, but not solid. Serve warm with crusty bread and a side salad.

(courtesy of Annie Barry of Annie's Restaurant in Ballydehob, Co. Cork)

Abbey Brie, Ham and Rocket Plait

Serves 4

> 400 g/14 oz puff pastry
> 350 g/12 oz cooked sliced ham
> 25 g/1 oz wholegrain mustard
> 200 g/7 oz sliced cooked leeks
> 175 g/6 oz Abbey Brie or other Brie cheese
> 25 g/1 oz rocket leaves
> 150 ml/¼ pt béchamel sauce
> 1 egg

> béchamel sauce:
> 150 ml/¼ pt milk
> 2 slices of onion
> 1 bay leaf
> 4 black peppercorns
> 15 g/½ oz butter
> 15 g/½ oz plain flour
> salt and freshly ground pepper

Make the béchamel sauce in advance. Put the milk, slices of onion, bay leaf and peppercorns in a small saucepan. Heat until almost boiling, then remove from heat, cover with a lid and leave for 8–10 minutes, then strain off the milk. Place the butter in a saucepan and melt over a gentle heat, and then stir in the flour. Cook for a further 1–2 minutes until the mixture becomes grainy in texture. Be careful not to brown it. Gradually stir in the warm milk, taking care to beat in the milk thoroughly each time you add it. When all the milk is used, simmer the sauce gently for 4–5 minutes, then add the seasoning. Allow to cool. To make the plait, roll out the pastry into a rectangular shape (20 cm × 100 cm/8 in. × 4 in.). Lay the pastry on a flat baking sheet. Place the ham in the centre of the pastry and spread the mustard over the ham, spoon the béchamel sauce down the centre of the ham and cover with the leeks. Lay the sliced cheese over the leeks and sprinkle the rocket on top. Cut the pastry on either side of the ham into wide strips. Fold the pastry over the top of the rocket one side after the other. Brush with beaten egg and place in a preheated oven and cook at 200°C/400°F/gas mark 6 for 30–40 minutes. Slice with a serrated edge knife.

(courtesy of Sarah Webb at the Gallic Kitchen)

Main Courses

Aubergine Wraps of Pine nuts, Spinach and Coolea Cheese with a Fresh Tomato, Thyme and Caper Sauce

Serves 4

4 medium aubergines
olive oil
400 g/14 oz spinach
60 g/2¼ oz pine nuts
4 sundried tomatoes
salt and pepper, to season
160 g/5 oz mature Coolea or mature Gouda

sauce:
6 tomatoes
2 cloves garlic
2 tsp small capers
2 sprigs thyme
45 ml/3 tbsp olive oil

Cut a slice from two sides of each aubergine lengthways and then cut the remaining flesh into three slices from each aubergine – four if they're very fat. You will need a few extra slices to allow for burning, accidents and sheer greed. Brush these slices lightly with olive oil and roast them in a hot oven until fully cooked and lightly coloured. Bring a large pot of water to the boil, drop in the spinach and cook it for one minute. Then remove it to a bowl of cold water to stop the cooking. When it is cooled, squeeze as much water as possible from the spinach and chop it coarsely. Toast the pine nuts lightly and chop them with a knife – you want them to be roughly chopped but not ground. A food processor will make too much powder even if you're careful. Another efficient method is to break them with a rolling pin. Chop the sundried tomatoes very finely and stir them into the spinach with the pine nuts and 30 ml/2 tbsp of olive oil, and season it well with salt and black pepper. Use a vegetable peeler to slice the cheese into thin shavings. Place the aubergines on a work surface, best-looking sides down. Place some of the spinach pine nut mix on one half of each slice, cover it with some shavings of cheese and fold over the other half of the aubergine to cover the filling. Place the aubergines on a parchment-lined oven tray and bake them in the oven at 180°C/350°F/gas mark 4, for 10 minutes or so, until the cheese has just melted into soft pillows, but hasn't become runny. Serve the wraps immediately.

To make the sauce, first peel the tomatoes. Cut a small cross into the base of each tomato and drop them into boiling water for a few seconds, then plunge them into cold water. The skins should slip off easily. Cut the tomatoes in half, scoop out the seeds and cut out any green stem. Chop the remaining flesh into small dice and put them in a small pan. Chop the garlic finely and add it to the pan with the capers, the leaves from the thyme sprigs and the olive oil. Heat the sauce gently until boiling, then simmer for one minute. Serve immediately.

From Paradiso Seasons by Denis Cotter published by Atrium in 2003. Denis Cotter is chef/proprietor of Café Paradiso in Cork.

An Irish Cheese Fondue Recipe

(courtesy of Bill Hogan of West Cork Natural Cheese)

A true cheese fondue must be made with thermophilic cheese. Gabriel, Desmond, Gruyère, Emmenthal, Appenzell are all suitable. A fondue may be cooked with one or any combination of these, depending on the flavour and effect that is desired.

Many white wines will compliment thermophilic cheeses. Light crisp wines like Riesling, Pinot Gris or Swiss Fendant work well. Avoid sharp or steely wines because they will sour the taste.

For serving 4 to 6 persons, cut at least one kilo of thermophilic cheese into half-thumb-sized chunks, removing the hard outer rind. Or use pre-grated cheese specially milled for fondue.

Heat a cup and a half of wine nearly to the boil, preferably in a ceramic pot, which may be pre-scented by rubbing with a dot of garlic.

Add half the cheese and stir slowly at first with a flat wooden spoon. Heat for eight to ten minutes, until the cheese suddenly begins to melt. As it dissolves, stir very briskly and lower the heat. To extend the fondue, add more cheese and wine. If it becomes too thick, pour in a bit more wine. Conversely, more cheese may be added if it gets too thin. The flame should be adjusted accordingly. Toss in a pinch of pepper at this point.

A small quantity of soft cheese may be amalgamated near the finish to achieve extra bouquet. Blend in a handful of your favourite Irish farmhouse cheese.

Traditionally fondue is eaten with small lumps of bread skewered on long forks or sticks. Each guest or family member gets an individual fork, tipped with bread then dipped in and twirled to gather the sauce. Until the pot is empty, someone must keep stirring. Instead of bread, try fondue sauce poured over lightly sauteed or steamed vegetables like mushrooms, onions, leeks, cauliflower or tomatoes, or try dipping raw or lightly cooked asparagus and broccoli spears in the hot fondue.

Salmon and Brie Fishcakes

Serves 2

> *225 g/8 oz cooked salmon, smoked haddock or white fish,*
> *   skin and bones removed*
> *115 g/4 oz mashed potatoes*
> *55 g/2 oz St Brendan or Abbey Brie, Cooleeney or St Killian,*
> *   cut into 8 cubes*
> *15 g/½ oz soft butter*
> *30 ml/2 tbsp chopped parsley*
> *salt and freshly ground black pepper*
> *1 beaten egg*
> *white breadcrumbs*
> *oil for frying*
> *lemon for garnish*

Combine the fish with the mashed potatoes, then beat in the parsley and butter. Season with salt and black pepper to taste. Divide the mixture into four, and incorporate a quarter of the cheese into each fishcake. Chill the fishcakes in the fridge for at least 4 hours. Before cooking, dip each fishcake in the egg, then the breadcrumbs. Fry the fishcakes in 2.5 cm/1 in. oil until golden brown. Drain briefly on kitchen towel, and serve immediately while still hot with a quarter of lemon. These fishcakes are fairly small. Those with large appetites should double the quantities.

Gratin of Cod with Smoked Cheese and Mustard

Serves 6

> *6 × 175 g/6 oz pieces of cod*
> *salt and freshly ground black pepper*
> *225 g/8 oz Baylough farmhouse smoked cheddar or other*
> *   smoked cheese*

15 ml/1 tbsp Dijon mustard
60 ml/4 tbsp cream

(You will need a buttered ovenproof dish 20 × 25 cm (8 × 10 in.).)

Preheat the oven to 180°C/350°F/gas mark 4. Season the fish with salt and pepper. Arrange the fillets in a single layer in an ovenproof dish. (It should be attractive enough to bring to the table.) Grate the cheese, mix with the mustard and cream and spread carefully over the fish. It can be prepared ahead and refrigerated at this point. Cook in the preheated oven for about 20 minutes or until the fish is cooked and the top is golden and bubbly. Flash under the grill if necessary.

Irish Farmhouse Fish Pie

Serves 4

> 700 g/1 lb 9 oz cod or haddock
> 850 ml/1½ pt milk
> 1 small onion, peeled
> 60 g/2¼ oz butter
> 60 g/2¼ oz flour
> 60 g/2¼ oz Mount Callan, Hegarty Farmhouse Cheddar or
>   other semi-hard cheese
> 3 small ripe tomatoes, skinned and chopped
> 2 hard-boiled eggs, shelled and chopped
> 2 tbsp parsley, finely chopped
> salt and freshly ground black pepper

> potato topping:
> 700 g/1 lb 9 oz potatoes, peeled weight
> 60 g/2¼ oz butter
> 60 ml/4 tbsp cream
> salt and freshly ground black pepper

Remove the bones from the fish. Place the fish, onion and milk together in a saucepan and bring gently to the boil over a low heat. Simmer for 2–3 minutes, then remove the pan from the heat and allow to cool. Strain off the milk from the fish through a sieve or colander and keep it for the sauce. Flake the fish, removing any skin and bone. Remove the onion. Melt the butter in a saucepan and stir in the flour. Let it cook for 2–3 minutes, then pour in the strained-off milk gradually, stirring well until the sauce comes to simmering point. Add the cheese, and cook for one minute, stirring continuously, until melted. Remove the pan from the heat and add the fish, chopped tomatoes, hard-boiled egg, parsley, a pinch of salt and some freshly ground pepper. Put the mixture into a pie dish. Meanwhile, cut the potatoes in chunks and boil until tender. Drain in a colander, return to pan and mash well. Mash in butter and cream and season with salt and pepper to taste. Cover the fish mixture with the mashed potato. Bake in a preheated oven 180°C/350°F/gas mark 4 for 25 minutes until cooked through and browned.

Scallop and Monkfish Gratin

Serves 4

garlic butter:
55 g/2 oz butter
2 crushed cloves of garlic
1 tbsp fresh parsley, chopped

white sauce:
25 g/1 oz butter
25 g/1 oz flour
150 ml/¼ pt milk

12 scallops prepared for cooking (ask your fishmonger to do this for you)
450 g/1 lb monkfish divided into 12 pieces
400 ml/14 fl oz dry white wine
60 ml/4 tbsp cream
salt and freshly ground pepper
225 g/8 oz grated Mount Callan, Knockanore or other semi-hard cheese
115 g/4 oz breadcrumbs

Mash the crushed garlic and parsley into the butter to make garlic butter. Melt the butter for the white sauce in a saucepan over a gentle heat, then add the flour and stir in thoroughly. Cook for 2 minutes, then add the milk gradually to make a thick white sauce. Remove from heat. Heat the garlic butter over a medium heat in a heavy-based frying pan. Pan fry the scallops and monkfish over a medium heat for 3–4 minutes, remove from pan, and keep warm. Add the white wine to the pan and reduce to half its volume. Add 120 ml/8 tbsp white sauce to the wine, season and finish by stirring in the cream. Pour into a shallow-sided ovenproof dish with the scallops and monkfish, and top with the cheese mixed with the breadcrumbs. Place under a hot grill, but be careful not to place it too near the flame, and grill for 3–4 minutes until bubbling and golden brown.

(courtesy of Trish O'Shea of O'Connor's Seafood Restaurant, Bantry, Co. Cork)

Breast of Chicken with a Bellingham Blue Cheese and Walnut Crust

Serves 4

    15 ml/1 tbsp olive oil
    1 tbsp chopped fresh sage
    4 skinless chicken breasts
    salt and pepper
    85 g/3 oz Bellingham Blue cheese or other blue cheese
    40 g/1½ oz walnut pieces

Preheat oven to 190°C/375°F/gas mark 5. Place the oil in a small bowl and stir in the sage. Place the chicken on a large baking tray and season with salt and pepper. Sprinkle the cheese and walnuts on top of the chicken, dividing the mixture evenly. Use a fork to lift sage from the oil. Divide the sage between the chicken breasts and drizzle the oil over the top. Bake for 25–30 minutes until the topping is golden and the chicken is completely cooked through. Serve with a green salad.

Chicken with Cooleeney Sauce

Serves 4

  1 kg/2 lb 4 oz chicken pieces
  pepper
  80 ml/3 fl oz chicken stock
  1 leek, thinly sliced
  125 ml/4 fl oz cream
  100 g/3½ oz Cooleeney or other Camembert-type cheese
  80 ml/5⅓ tbsp soured cream
  80 ml/5⅓ tbsp dry vermouth
  55 g/2 oz walnut pieces

Sprinkle chicken with pepper and cook in an oven 200°C/400°F/gas mark 6 for 25 minutes, turning once. Pour in stock and bake for another 10 minutes. Drain stock into a saucepan and keep the chicken warm. To make sauce, heat stock in a saucepan, add leek, cream and Cooleeney and stir until the cheese melts. Simmer for 3–4 minutes before stirring in soured cream and vermouth. Place chicken on warm serving dish and pour over sauce and sprinkle with walnuts. Excellent served with brown rice and a green vegetable.

Lamb Chops with Sheep's Cheese

Serves 4

  200 g/7 oz Knockalara sheep's cheese or other similar cheese
  fresh basil and parsley, chopped
  4 tomatoes
  8 lamb cutlets
  30 ml/2 tbsp virgin olive oil
  salt and freshly ground pepper
  2 cloves garlic, crushed

Preheat the oven to 220°C/425°F/gas mark 7. Mix basil, parsley and sheep's cheese, broken into pieces. Cut tomatoes in half and cover with salt and pepper. Sauté the chops in the olive oil in a heavy frying pan over a high heat for about 2 minutes on each side. Put the meat and tomatoes in a casserole. Rub in the crushed garlic, salt and pepper. Pour the cheese and herbs into the casserole. Place in the preheated oven for approximately 10 minutes until the cheese is bubbling and melted. Serve immediately with French bread and a green salad.

Beef Stew with Guiness and Cheese and Mustard Dumplings

Serves 4

900 g/2 lb good stewing steak, cut in bite-size pieces
45 ml/3 tbsp oil
3 medium-sized onions, finely sliced
2 cloves of garlic, crushed
12.5 g/½ oz dark brown sugar
25 g/1 oz plain flour
450 ml/16 fl oz Guinness
425 ml/¾ pt beef stock
5 ml/1 tsp white wine vinegar
4 bay leaves
1 tbsp mixed herbs
salt and freshly ground black pepper

dumplings:
225 g/8 oz self-raising flour
115 g/4 oz shredded suet
25 g/1 oz Mount Callan cheddar or other semi-hard cheese
5 ml/1 tsp Lakeshore Strong Irish Mustard or other strong mustard
pinch of salt
freshly ground black pepper

Set aside a large casserole dish. Heat the oil in a heavy-based frying pan and fry the pieces of meat a few at a time, until browned, then remove with a slotted spoon and place in the casserole. Slowly fry the onions in the remaining oil until they begin to brown. Add the garlic and sugar, stir well and cook for a further 2–3 minutes. Be careful not to burn the onions. Stir in the flour and cook for 2 minutes, stirring occasionally. Gradually pour in the Guinness and stock, stirring continuously and bring to the boil. Pour over the meat in the casserole and add the vinegar, bay leaves, mixed herbs and salt and pepper. Heat the casserole on the hob until it begins to bubble, then cover and place in an oven preheated to 150°C/300°F/gas mark 2 for 3 hours. To make the dumplings, mix the flour, suet, grated cheese, mustard, salt and pepper together, then add 60 ml/4 tbsp water to bind to a stiff dough. Shape the dough into 8 similar balls. Add to the stew after 2¼ hours, gently pushing the balls of dough down into the liquid, and cook for a further 45 minutes.

Boilie Burgers

Serves 4

450 g/1 lb prime beef, minced
1 onion, finely sliced
1 clove of garlic, finely chopped
salt and pepper
30 ml/2 tbsp Lakeshore Whole Grain Irish Mustard or other whole grain mustard
4 rounds of goats', or cows' Boilie cheese

Mix the mince, onion, garlic, mustard, salt and pepper together in a bowl. Shape mixture into 4 burgers. Make a hole in the centre of each of them and fill with a Boilie. Reshape to cover Boilie. Grill or fry for 5–6 minutes on both sides. Serve immediately.

Fillet Steak with Blue Cheese Topping

Serves 4

100 g/3½ oz Crozier Blue or other blue cheese, rind removed
25 g/1 oz softened butter
55 g/2 oz walnuts, chopped
salt and pepper to taste
4 fillet steaks

Crumble the cheese, and mix with the softened butter and chopped walnuts. Season with salt and pepper. Grill steaks as normal, then spread the topping on the steaks and press it down well. Grill for a minute or until the topping is bubbling and melting. Serve immediately.

Carrigaline Thatched Pork Chop

Serves 4

 4 pork loin chops
 salt and freshly ground black pepper
 2 cooking apples, peeled, cored and chopped
 45 ml/3 tbsp water
 125 g/4½ oz Carrigaline or Knockanore cheese, grated or
  finely chopped

Season chops and grill for 10–15 minutes on each side. Meanwhile, place apples in a saucepan with the water. Cover and cook gently until the apples form a thick pulp. Mix in half the cheese. Spread the apple mixture over the cooked chops. Sprinkle the remaining cheese over the top. Return the chops to the grill and cook until the cheese melts and begins to brown.

Gabriel, Leek and Smoked Ham Bake

Serves 4

 4 medium leeks, trimmed and washed
 4 large slices of smoked ham
 85 g/3 oz butter
 55 g/2 oz plain flour
 600 ml/1 pt milk
 115 g/4 oz Gabriel, Desmond or other hard cheese, finely grated
 a little extra grated cheese for the topping
 5 ml/1 tsp Lakeshore Strong Irish Mustard or other strong
  mustard
 2 tbsp chopped parsley

Lightly poach the leeks until tender. Remove the leeks from the pan, and reserve the liquid. Cut each leek and each slice of ham into two pieces. Wrap each piece of leek with ham and place in an ovenproof dish. Meanwhile make the cheese sauce. Melt the butter in a small saucepan, stir in the flour and cook for two minutes. Gradually add the milk, stirring continuously, and 100 ml/3½ fl oz of the reserved leek liquid. Cook for a further 5 minutes, then add the cheese, the mustard and half the parsley, stir and remove from heat. Spoon the sauce over the leeks and ham and sprinkle with a little extra grated cheese. Cook at 200°C/400°F/gas mark 6 for 15 minutes. Serve with a sprinkling of chopped parsley.

(courtesy of James and Mary Hegarty of Bantry, Co. Cork)

Milleens with Pasta

Serves 4

> *225 g/8 oz grated Milleens or other washed-rind cheese*
> *300 ml/½ pt cream*
> *a handful of fresh sage leaves*
> *350 g/12 oz tagliatelle*

Place the sage leaves in a saucepan and pour in the cream. Warm the cream, but be careful not to overheat. Allow to sit in a warm place until the cream has absorbed the flavour of the sage and then strain. Add the Milleens and, if necessary, warm gently and stir until the cheese has completely melted. Cook the tagliatelle until al dente. Pour the creamy sauce over the tagliatelle, mix and serve.

This dish stands alone, but can be rendered more substantial by the addition of ham, which has been cut into strips of the same width as the pasta or alternatively some white or smoked fish or chopped cooked spinach, or some lightly cooked fennel.

Potatoes

Leek and Smoked Cheese Mash

Serves 4

    800 g/1 lb 12 oz floury potatoes
    60 g/2¼ oz butter
    150 ml/¼ pt milk
    salt and pepper
    1 leek, finely chopped
    2 cloves of garlic, finely chopped
    100 g/3½ oz Smoked Gubbeen or other mild smoked cheese,
        diced into small pieces

Boil, then mash the potatoes and add the butter and milk, and salt and pepper to taste. While the potatoes are boiling, slice the leek in half lengthways almost to the base and wash it carefully under running water. Chop the leek finely and fry it with the garlic in a third of the butter for a few minutes until the leek is beginning to soften, but retaining its colour. Just before you serve the mash, stir in the leek and the smoked cheese. It's best if the cheese only partly melts.

From The Café Paradiso Cookbook *by Denis Cotter published by Atrium in 1999. Denis Cotter is Chef/Proprietor of the Café Paradiso in Cork.*

Crunchy Baylough Garlic and Herb Farmhouse Potato Bake

Serves 4

> 700 g/1 lb 9 oz potatoes, peeled
> 55 g/2 oz Baylough garlic and herb or similar semi-hard
>   cheese, grated
> 1 medium-sized onion, peeled and finely chopped
> 1 clove garlic, peeled and crushed
> 2 tbsp chopped parsley
> salt and black pepper
> 55 g/2 oz butter, melted

Grate the potatoes coarsely, place in a colander and rinse excess starch from them with cold water. Dry well using a clean tea towel. In a bowl, mix together the potatoes, cheese, onion, garlic and parsley. Season well. Pile mixture into a buttered shallow ovenproof dish and brush top with the melted butter. Cover dish with tin foil and place in a preheated oven 200°C/400°F/gas mark 6 for 45 minutes. Remove the foil and bake for a further 20 minutes approximately, until the potatoes are cooked through and the top is crisp and golden. Cut into sections and serve hot.

Durrus and Potato Melt

Serves 4

> 900 g/2 lb waxy potatoes, cubed
> 1 small Durrus or 400 g/14 oz portion, rind removed, cubed
> 2 onions, finely chopped
> 200 g/7 oz bacon rashers, cut into small pieces
> 250 g/9 oz tub crème fraîche
> black pepper and salt

Steam or parboil the potatoes until just soft. Gently cook the onions and bacon in a covered pan. Put the potatoes, onions, bacon and cheese in a buttered shallow oven dish.

Add salt and pepper and pour on the crème fraîche, mixing gently. Bake at 180°C/350°F/gas mark 4 for 15–20 minutes. Stir gently after 10 minutes. Serve with green salad and red wine.

Baked Potato with Tuna Fish and Cheese

Serves 2

> 2 large baking potatoes
> 1 × 190 g/6½ oz tin tuna in oil
> 2 spring onions, washed, trimmed and finely chopped
> 60 ml/4 tbsp mayonnaise
> 55 g/2 oz Durrus or other washed-rind cheese, grated

Bake the potatoes on a baking tray in an oven preheated to 200°C/400°F/gas mark 6 for 1 hour. They can be tested with a skewer to make sure they are properly cooked. Meanwhile mix the tuna, mayonnaise and spring onion together. Remove the baked potatoes from the oven, split lengthways, top with the tuna mixture, then the grated cheese. Place under a hot grill for 3–4 minutes until brown and bubbling. Serve immediately.

Lavistown Cheese and Spuds

Boil some potatoes (peeled or not as you wish) until just done or use some cold leftover ones. Cut them into chunks and then fry them in a non-stick pan with a couple of tablespoons of olive oil until they are crisp and brown. Season with plenty of salt and pepper. Sprinkle plenty of diced Lavistown cheese over the potatoes in the pan and put the whole lot under a hot grill until melted, golden and bubbling. Serve immediately. Alternative cheese suggestion: any semi-soft or Cheddar-type cheese.

Olivia Goodwillie, maker of Lavistown cheese describes her recipe as 'A very simple dish that surpasses the sum of its parts'.

Bread

Brioche of Cratloe Hills Sheep's Cheese

Serves 4–6

brioche dough:
225 g/8 oz strong white flour
1 sachet instant dried yeast
1 tsp salt
15 g/½ oz caster sugar
2 medium eggs, beaten
115 g/4 oz butter, softened

filling:
115 g/4 oz Cratloe Hills sheep's cheese or similar cheese,
   grated or finely chopped
1 small red onion, diced
1 small clove of garlic, crushed
2 leaves of basil, chopped
2 medium tomatoes, peeled, seeded and diced
a little butter

Make up the brioche dough first. Mix flour, instant yeast, salt
and sugar. Add beaten egg and softened butter and mix to a
dough. Knead by hand, with a mixer, or in a food processor
for about 5 minutes. Place dough in a greased bowl. Cover
and leave to rise for one hour. Punch the dough down, knead
again, then divide into 4–6 pieces. Roll out each piece into a
round of 12.5 cm/5 in. square. Make the topping for the
cheese by cooking the onion, garlic, basil and tomatoes
together in a little butter. Divide the cheese into 4–6 portions
and place one piece in the centre of each square and spoon
the topping over the cheese. Moisten the edges of the bread
and close up like a drawstring purse. Brush with milk and

bake on a greased baking sheet at 200°C/400°F/gas mark 6 for about 12 to 15 minutes until nicely browned and cooked through.

Cheesy Loaf

Makes 1 loaf

$^1/_3$ oz/8 g fresh yeast (or $^1/_4$ or 7 g sachet of dried yeast)
25 g/1 oz caster sugar
35 ml/2$^2/_3$ tbsp tepid water
3 free range eggs
225 g/8 oz strong white flour
pinch of salt
115 g/4 oz soft butter
butter for greasing bowl
1 egg, whisked
115 g/4 oz Gabriel, Hegarty Farmhouse Cheddar or other
   semi-hard cheese, finely grated

Dissolve yeast and sugar in water in a mixing bowl and add 2 whisked eggs beating all the time. Add the flour and salt and mix to a stiff dough. When the mixture is smooth, beat in the butter in small pieces. Place in a bowl greased with butter, cover and put overnight in the fridge. Knead ¾ of cheese into dough, then put into a well-buttered loaf tin. Whisk an egg and brush the loaf with half of it, and stand in a warm place until doubled in size. Brush with the remaining whisked egg and sprinkle with the rest of the cheese. Bake in an oven preheated to 180°C/350°F/gas mark 4 for 35 minutes. Remove from tin and serve with some freshly made soup.

(courtesy of James and Mary Hegarty of Bantry, Co. Cork)

Cheesy Potato Cakes

Serves 2

> 225 g/8 oz potatoes
> 55 g/2 oz Baylough, Mount Callan, Hegarty Farmhouse or
>   other cheddar, grated
> ½ tsp salt
> 15 g/½ oz butter
> 55 g/2 oz (approx.) flour

Boil the potatoes. Drain and mash to remove all lumps. Add
the cheese, salt and butter, and work in as much flour as the
potatoes will absorb. This will vary according to the moist-
ness of the potatoes. Turn onto a floured surface and knead
lightly. Shape into a rectangle and cut into 4. Fry until lightly
browned on each side. This will take 10–15 minutes. Serve
immediately as part of a breakfast fry-up or as a tea-time
snack.

Cashel Blue Sage Scones

Serves 6

> 450 g/1 lb flour
> 1 egg
> 225 g/8 oz Cashel Blue cheese or other blue cheese
> 300 ml/½ pint yoghurt or sour milk or buttermilk
> 2 tsp sage
> 2 tsp cream of tartar
> 1 tsp bread soda
> 1 tsp salt
> a little freshly ground black pepper
> pinch of cayenne pepper
> 1 egg whisked with a pinch of salt for glaze
> sesame seeds for sprinkling on top of scones

Preheat oven to 250°C/475°F/gas mark 9. Put the flour,
sage, cream of tartar, bread soda, salt and black and
cayenne pepper in a bowl. Crumble the cheese into small

pieces, and add to the dry ingredients with the egg and yoghurt. Mix to a soft dough. Turn out onto a floured board. Pat or roll out to about 2.5 cm/1 in. thick and cut into scones with a floured 6 cm/2½ in. scone-cutter. Place on a greased baking tray. Brush with whisked egg and sprinkle with sesame seeds. Cook for 15–20 minutes until golden brown.

Herby Cheese Scones

Serves 4

> *350 g/12 oz self-raising flour*
> *1 tsp baking powder*
> *pinch of salt*
> *2 eggs*
> *15 ml/1 tbsp oil*
> *280 ml/9½ fl oz milk*
> *85 g/3 oz Knockanore, Hegarty Farmhouse or other semi-hard cheese, grated*
> *2 tbsp freshly chopped mixed chives and parsley*

Sieve the flour, baking powder and salt into a mixing bowl, and add the egg whisked with the oil and the milk, except for 30 ml/2 tbsp milk which should be reserved. Add the cheese, chives and parsley and mix all the ingredients together thoroughly with a wooden spoon. Place the mixture on a well-floured board and flatten to a thickness of 2.5 cm/1 in. Use a floured 6 cm/2½ in. scone-cutter to cut 8 scones. Whisk the other egg and mix with the reserved milk. Brush the scones with this and place on a baking tray greased with butter. Put the baking tray in an oven preheated to 220°C/425°F/gas mark 7 for 15–18 minutes until golden brown. Serve warm with butter.

Sweets & Savouries

Chocolate Goats' Cheese Nests

Serves 4

> 8 chocolate nests or cups (available in supermarkets)
> 225 g/8 oz Ardsallagh soft goats' cheese or other creamy soft
>   goats' cheese
> 1 fresh lemon
> icing sugar
> chocolate for garnish

Zest and juice the lemon. Mash the goats' cheese with a fork
and then add the lemon juice and zest. Add icing sugar to
taste (approx. 15 ml/1 tbsp to 200 g/7 oz cheese). Spoon
the cheese mixture into the chocolate nests. Grate or curl
chocolate on top.

Alternative serving suggestion: brandy snap nests or
sweet pastry nests with orange juice or crystallized ginger
and ground ginger.

Blue Cheese and Apple Strudel

Serves 6–8

> 350 g/12 oz made weight puff pastry (can be bought frozen,
>   then defrosted)
> flour for dusting
> 250 g/9 oz Cashel Blue or other blue cheese
> 500 g/1 lb 2 oz cooking apples, peeled, cored and chopped
> 100 g/3½ oz brown breadcrumbs
> 55 g/1¾ oz chopped walnuts
> beaten egg to glaze

Set the oven to 200°C/400°F/gas mark 6. Roll out the pastry as thinly as possible, on a lightly floured surface, to a rectangle measuring 50 × 40 cm, 20 in. × 16 in. Mix together the cheese, apples, breadcrumbs and walnuts. Spread the mixture over the pastry, leaving a border of 2.5 cm/1 in. Carefully roll up the pastry, tucking in the edges, to form a neat roll. Place the roll on a dampened baking sheet, brush with beaten egg and bake it for about 30 minutes until lightly browned. Remove the baking sheet from the oven and place the strudel on a serving dish. Serve hot or warm with cream.

Soused St Brendan Brie

Serves 4

    250 g/9 oz St Brendan Brie, St Killian or Cooleeney
    150 ml/¼ pt dry white wine
    100 g/3½ oz softened butter
    15–30 ml/1–2 tbsp brandy
    cayenne and black pepper to taste
    25 g/1 oz fine toasted breadcrumbs
    2 tbsp finely chopped parsley

Remove rind from the cheese and cut into wedges. Soak overnight in wine. Drain well. Cream cheese thoroughly with the butter, peppers and brandy. Put back into the original shape of the cheese. Coat top and bottom with the breadcrumbs and coat sides with the parsley. Chill for 2 hours. Arrange on a serving dish. Serve with cheese biscuits or toast. Alternatively the mixture may be placed in individual serving pots and topped with crumbs and parsley.

Blue Cheese Cheesecake

Serves 6

base:
115 g/4 oz butter
175 g/6 oz water biscuits, finely crushed
garlic salt
black pepper

filling:
200 g/7 oz full fat cream cheese
2 eggs, separated
5 ml/1 tsp French mustard
250 ml/½ pt cream
garlic salt
black pepper
175 g/6 oz blue cheese, crumbled
12 g/½ oz gelatine
60 ml/4 tbsp water

garnish:
toasted almonds

To make base, melt the butter over a low heat. Add biscuit crumbs and season. Mix well until butter has been absorbed. Press this mixture into the base of an oiled 25 cm/10 in. loose-bottomed cake tin. For the filling, put cream cheese, egg yolks, French mustard, cream, garlic salt, pepper and crumbled blue cheese into a bowl. Whisk until smooth. Mix gelatine with water in a heatproof bowl and allow to stand in hot water until the gelatine is completely dissolved. Cool slightly and whisk into the cheese mixture. Allow to stand until it reaches the point of setting. Whisk egg whites until stiff. Fold into the cheese mixture carefully but thoroughly. Pour into the tin and refrigerate for 6 hours. Remove cheesecake from tin. Coat the sides with toasted almonds. Decorate and serve chilled.

(courtesy of the National Dairy Council)

The Cheeseboard

Cheese can be selected for a cheeseboard in a variety of ways. The classic way is to choose three or four cheeses in peak condition, which differ from each other in strength, taste, texture and colour. Select from different cheese groups – blue, washed rind, goats', hard or soft. Contrasting shaped cheeses can also add interest. Another way of creating a cheeseboard is to have variations on the same theme, for example a selection of washed-rind cheeses or goats' cheeses, where the similarity will make it possible to savour their differences better. The best and most effective option, however, can be to have one perfectly ripened cheese on its own.

Fresh crusty or speciality bread or fresh high quality cheese biscuits should accompany the cheeseboard. Fruit such as pears, apples and figs goes well with cheese, but not citrus fruit. Sweet chutneys, hazelnuts, walnuts or almonds in their shell, spring onions, watercress, olives and celery also complement cheese. Honey is a good accompaniment to blue cheese. The cheeseboard can be decorated by serving the cheese on a bed of leaves or with wild flowers and herbs.

List of Cheeses

ABBEY BRIE is made in mild blue, naturally smoked and plain versions by the Abo Cheese Company with pasteurized cows' milk and vegetarian rennet in Co. Laois. They also make St Canice feta using pasteurized ewes' milk and vegetarian rennet.

ARDRAHAN a semi-soft washed rind cheese made using pasteurized cows' milk and vegetarian rennet in Co. Cork.

ARDSALLAGH SOFT GOATS' CHEESE a soft full-fat, mild cream cheese made using pasteurized goats' milk and vegetarian rennet in Co. Cork.

BAYLOUGH FARMHOUSE CHEESE a hard-pressed Cheddar-type cheese. It is made in plain, oak smoked, garlic and herb, smoked garlic and herb and garlic versions using raw cows' milk and vegetarian rennet in Co. Tipperary.

BEENOSKEE a mature hard cheese made by Dingle Peninsula Cheese. There is also a version made using seaweed. It is made using raw cows' milk and vegetarian rennet in Co. Kerry.

BELLINGHAM BLUE a traditional semi-hard blue cheese made using raw cows' milk and vegetarian rennet in Co. Louth.

BOILIE a soft fresh cream cheese made in two versions, one made using pasteurized cows' milk and the other using pasteurized goats' milk, and vegetarian rennet in Co. Cavan.

CAHILLS FARMHOUSE CHEESE a range of flavoured Cheddars made using pasteurized cows' milk and vegetarian rennet. Flavours include Irish herbs, porter, whiskey and chives.

CARRIGALINE a semi-firm cheese made in natural, and herb and garlic versions using pasteurized cows' milk and vegetarian rennet in Co. Cork.

CASHEL BLUE a semi-soft mild blue cheese made using pasteurized cows' milk and vegetarian rennet by J & L Grubb Ltd in Co. Tipperary.

CLONMORE a Gouda-style cheese made using pasteurized goats' milk and vegetarian rennet in Co. Cork.

COOLEA made to a Gouda recipe using pasteurized cows' milk and vegetarian rennet in Co. Cork.

COOLEENEY a Camembert-style cheese made using raw or pasteurized cows' milk and vegetarian rennet in Co. Tipperary.

CORBETSTOWN GOATS' CHEESE a natural-rind semi-hard cheese made using pasteurized goats' milk and vegetarian rennet.

CORLEGGY a natural-rind hard cheese made using pasteurized goats' milk and vegetarian rennet in Co. Cavan.

CRATLOE HILLS a semi-hard maturing to hard sheep's cheese made using pasteurized ewes' milk and vegetarian rennet in Co. Clare.

CROZIER BLUE a semi-soft mild blue cheese made using pasteurized sheep's milk and vegetarian rennet by J & L Grubb Ltd in Co. Tipperary.

DILLISKUS a semi-hard cheese flavoured with hand-picked dillisk, a dark red seagrass, made using raw cows' milk and vegetarian rennet by Dingle Peninsula Cheese in Co. Kerry.

DRUMLIN a firm cheese with a loose texture and natural rind made using raw cows' milk and vegetarian rennet. Flavours include plain, beech-smoked, green peppercorn, cumin and garlic.

DUNBARRA a soft white moulded cheese made by Cooleeney Farmhouse Cheese. It is made in plain, garlic, and dill and pepper versions using pasteurized cows' milk and vegetarian renent in Co. Tipperary.

DURRUS a semi-soft washed rind cheese made from raw cows' milk and standard traditional rennet in Co. Cork.

GABRIEL and **DESMOND** thermophilic extra hard cheeses made using raw summer cows' milk and vegetarian rennet in Co. Cork.

GORTNAMONA a soft white moulded goats' milk cheese made using pasteurized goats' milk and vegetarian rennet in Co. Tipperary.

GUBBEEN a semi-soft washed rind cheese made using pasteurized cows' milk and vegetarian rennet in Co. Cork.

HEGARTY'S FARMHOUSE CHEDDAR a mature clothbound Cheddar made using pasteurized cows' milk and vegetarian rennet in Co. Cork.

KILCUMMIN a traditional semi-hard plain cheese made using raw cows' milk and vegetarian rennet by Dingle Peninsula Cheese in Co. Kerry.

KNOCKALARA a firm sheep's cheese made using pasteurized ewes' milk and vegetarian rennet in Co. Waterford. They also make Waterford feta.

KNOCKANORE softer than Cheddar and harder than Gouda and is made in plain, oak smoked, herb and garlic, black pepper and chive, and mature red versions using raw cows' milk and vegetarian rennet in Co. Waterford.

LAVISTOWN a hard Cheddar-style cheese, which crumbles and is less compact than Cheddar. It is made using pasteurized cows' milk and vegetarian rennet in Co. Kilkenny.

MAIGHEAN a strong-flavoured soft cheese made using raw cows' milk and vegetarian rennet in Co. Tipperary.

MILLEENS a washed-rind cheese made using pasteurized cows' milk and vegetarian rennet in Co. Cork.

MINE GABHAR a delicate goats' milk cheese with a mottled natural rind and fine blue and white bloom made using raw goats' milk and vegetarian rennet.

MOUNT CALLAN a traditional mature Cheddar made using raw cows' milk and standard traditional rennet in Co. Clare.

OISIN FARMHOUSE CHEESE make a range of organic goats' cheeses using pasteurized goats' milk and vegetarian rennet in Co. Limerick.

ST BRENDAN BRIE made using pasteurized cows' milk and vegetarian rennet by Carrigbyrne Farmhouse in Co. Wexford.

ST GALL a hard-pressed Swiss-type cheese made using raw cows' milk and standard traditional rennet in Co. Cork.

ST KILLIAN a Camembert-style cheese made using pasteurized cows' milk and vegetarian rennet by Carrigbyrne Farmhouse in Co. Wexford.

ST TOLA make a range of organic cheeses using raw goats' milk and vegetarian rennet in Co. Clare.

WICKLOW BLUE a mild, creamy, blue-veined cheese made from pasteurized cows' milk and vegetarian rennet in Co. Wicklow.

For further information, consult the Bord Bia website:

www.foodisland.com

CáIS Irish Farmhouse Cheesemakers Association is a voluntary association made up of over forty cheesemakers. Independently run and managed by the cheesemakers themselves, CáIS provides essential information, knowledge and networking opportunities for members. CáIS co-promotes Irish Farmhouse Cheese as a full range to over twenty markets worldwide. For further information, please go to:

www.irishcheese.ie

Acknowledgements

I would like to thank the following cheese makers for providing and letting me use their recipes: Patrick Berridge of Carrigbyrne Farmhouse; Tom Biggane of Clonmore; Maja Binder of Dingle Peninsula Cheese; Mark Brodie of Boilie; Mary Burns of Ardrahan; Silke Cropp of Corleggy; Giana Ferguson of Gubbeen; Sean and Deirdre Fitzgerald of Cratloe Hills; Siobhan Garvey of St Tola; Jeffa Gill of Durrus; Olivia Goodwillie of Lavistown; Jane and Louis Grubb of J & L Grubb Ltd; Dan Hegarty of Hegarty Farmhouse; John Hempenstall of Wicklow Blue; Bill Hogan of the West Cork Natural Cheese Company; Pat Hyland of the Abo Cheese Company; Anne Keating of Baylough; Eamonn Lonergan of Knockanore; Lucy Hayes of Mount Callan; Pat and Breda Maher of Cooleeney; Jane Murphy of Ardsallagh; Pat O'Farrell of Carrigaline; Gudrun Shinnick of St Gall; Agnes Schliebitz of Knockalara; Veronica Steele of Milleens; Peter Thomas of Bellingham Blue; Rochus Van der Vaard of Oisin Farmhouse; Dick Willems of Coolea. I would also like to thank: Myrtle Allen; Annie Barry; Edward Twomey of the Clonakilty Blackpudding Co.; Ann Conner; Ben Russell; Denis Cotter; James and Mary Hegarty; Clodagh McKenna; Rory O'Connell; Trish O'Shea; Carmel Somers; Edward Twomey of the Clonakilty Blackpudding Co. and Sarah Webb for giving me recipes; Val Manning of Manning's Emporium, Ballylickey; Kevin Sheridan of Sheridan's Cheesemongers, Dublin; and Fiona Burke of Bantry Friday Market for providing wonderful cheese; Matilda Bevan and Monika Kemper for research; Colette Shannon; Una Fitzgibbon; Mary Morrissey and Eimear O'Donnell of Bord Bia; and finally my husband, Andrew Russell, of the Somerville Press, for continuous help and support with this book.

Cheese Shops in London & Scotland

Irish farmhouse cheeses can be found in most good cheese shops throughout the UK and selected branches of Waitrose and Sainsbury's. The following is a list of shops in London and Scotland, which stock a range of Irish farmhouse cheese.

LONDON

Bayley & Sage
60 High Street
London SW19 8EE
Tel: 020 8946 9904

Blue Bird
350 Kings Road
Chelsea
London SW3 5UU
Tel: 020 7559 1173

Fresh and Wild
210 Westbourne Grove
London W11 2RH
Tel: 020 7229 1063

5 other branches:

Fresh and Wild
294 Old Street
London EC1V 9FR
Tel: 020 7250 1708

Fresh and Wild
32–40 Stoke Newington
  Church Street
London N16 0LU
Tel: 020 7254 2332

Fresh and Wild
49 Parkway
London NW1 7PN
Tel: 020 7428 7575

Fresh and Wild
305 Lavender Hill
London SW11 1LN
Tel: 020 7585 1488

Fresh and Wild
69–75 Brewer Street
London W1F 9US
Tel: 020 7434 3179

Fortnum and Mason
181 Piccadilly
London W1A 1ER
Tel: 020 7734 8040

Harrods
Knightsbridge
London SW1X 7XL
Tel: 020 7730 1234

Harvey Nichols
109 Knightsbridge
London SW1X 7RJ
Tel: 020 7235 5020

Jeroboams
96 Holland Park Avenue
London W11 3RB
Tel: 020 7727 9359

Jeroboams
51 Elizabeth Street
London SW1W 9PP
Tel: 020 7823 5623

Hamish Johnston
48 Northcote Road
London SW11 1PA
Tel: 020 7738 0741

C. Lidgate
110 Holland Park Avenue
London W11 3RB
Tel: 020 7727 8243

Mise-en-Place
21 Battersea Rise
London SW11 1HG
Tel: 020 7228 3394

Mortimer & Bennett
13 Turnham Green Terrace
London W4 1RG
Tel: 020 8995 4145

Neal's Yard Dairy
17 Shorts Gardens
London WC2H 9UP
Tel: 020 7240 5700

Neal's Yard Dairy
6 Park Street
London SE1 9AB
Tel: 020 7645 3554

Paxton & Whitfield
93 Jermyn Street
London SW1Y 6JE
Tel: 020 7930 0259

Rosslyn Delicatessen
56 Rosslyn Hill
London NW3 1ND
Tel: 020 7794 9210

Selfridges Ltd
400 Oxford Street
London W1A 1AB
Tel: 08708 377377

Tom's Deli
226 Westbourne Grove
London W11 2RH
Tel: 020 7221 8818

Villandry Food & Wine
170 Great Portland Street
London W1W 5QB
Tel: 020 7631 3131

SCOTLAND

I.J. Mellis Cheesemonger
30A Victoria Street
Edinburgh EH1 2JW
Tel: 0131 226 6215

I.J. Mellis Cheesemonger
492 Western Road
Glasgow G12 8EW
Tel: 0141 339 8998